My PUG is an Asshole

Matt Shaw

Introduction

When I was growing up I always wanted a dog. We had cats, a couple of hamsters, a chinchilla, some fish and - as far as I can remember - that was it. No dog despite my desire. In fact, living with my mum and dad, the closest I got to changing the "no dog" situation was when I was seventeen years old and met a girl called Gill but that's another story - one that is also filled with bitter resentment, loathing and regret. Let's move on.

I don't know why I wanted a dog. To my recollection my friends didn't have one so it's not like I went around their house and fell in love with the idea of a doggy companion. I was driven to school by my mum so I didn't meet any dog-walkers on the way to and from. I never went to the park to play on the swings, another place you might potentially meet dogs (and their owners). In fact, the only dog that I really knew growing up was Carla, my neighbour's black lab. She was friendly enough but spent most of the time sleeping whenever I was round playing with Christopher or Claire, so it's not as though I even formed a bond with dogs there. So, yeah, I don't know why I wanted a dog, I just did. Sadly for me, my mum and dad didn't.

I moved out of my mum and dad's when I was in my twenties. Or rather I moved out of their house (for the second time) when I was in my twenties. The first time was a false start and I made a mess of things and had to go crawling back. Mind you, the first time I moved out, I was not in a position to own a dog either - what with working full time and not having much money. Now if you're one of those people who questions why that should matter, let me just stop the book right here and call you an arsehole. Dogs crave company almost as much as the lonely men who hire ladies by the hour. They do not like being left alone all day feeling sorry for themselves and unloved (actually, that sounds like me growing up) and as for money - owning a dog is expensive. *I know that now.* If you don't have a spare £100.00 a month, put this book down now and walk away. You are not ready to own a dog and if you think that sounds excessive - keep in mind I own a pug. Her insurance is £40 a month (for the best we can get because veterinary bills can be expensive) and she eats about £30 of normal dog food in a month. Add to that the cost of the toys and the treats and you're looking at £100 a month at the minimum (for a small dog) and don't kid yourself in pretending you won't want to buy your doggie treats and toys. Anyway we're getting ahead of ourselves… I wasn't in a place to buy a dog the first time I moved from my parents' house and nor was I in a place to buy a dog when I married my first wife. I was still struggling financially and I was working ridiculous hours each day. In fact, I wasn't ready to buy a dog until I was in my mid-thirties so let's fast forward to then and get things on the move, shall we? Oh, actually, a quick word before we do - please do not go into this book thinking it is a Marley & Me story where I get a naughty dog, grow to love it and then - after many adventures together - am crushed when it dies. At the time of writing, the mutt is very much alive and well, only a few feet away from me - licking this bone as though it's the juiciest piece of meat ever. Stupid dog. Surely she must know there is no *actual* meat on it and it would be tastier if there was? Whatever. Keeps her quiet and that's good enough for me.

Chapter One

Bored.

We have skipped a lot of my life and as such you've missed a lot of important information so, to make things easy for you and to avoid confusion, I'll give you a recap similar to when you tune into your favourite weekly television show.

Previously on Matt's Life:

Matt binned his wife. She wasn't good for him and he wasn't good for her. For a while he drifted the dating scene like a cool cat (if a cool cat went home, alone and completely unloved despite having paid a fortune for the dates) before eventually finding The One. Or rather The One "at the moment" (insert cheeky wink here later). A whirlwind romance and the girl moved in after three months. By Christmas they were engaged and by August, married. Not that some of her family regard them as married for no one was actually invited to the wedding but still... They were married. Matt's career also took off in this time. Finally, his dream of becoming a full time author came to fruition and he disappeared from society - locking himself in his home day in and day out, writing book after book. The whole time thinking, *God I'm lonely.* And that's when it hit him... A thought popping into his head completely out of the blue. A thought which - had this been a cartoon - would have been illustrated by a lightbulb appearing next to his head. *I could get a dog.*

And that's where we are now.

I was sitting at my computer, bored one day. I have a cat still but she doesn't hang out with me and Wife Number Two was at work. I was in-between writing projects and none of my author buddies were online to chat with. This is when I am at my most dangerous for I usually reach for my credit card and spend cash on pointless tat in an effort to cheer myself up. I don't know why I am programmed this way, I just am. I like presents and, if I have to purchase them for myself then so be it! Anyway, instead of heading to Amazon like I usually do, I zoned out momentarily and - when I came back to reality - I had Googled puppies. To be more precise, I had Googled Pug puppies in my local area. I hit return and - oh my days - the cute pictures that filled my computer screen... Instantly I was in love. That night, The Wife came home and we were chatting away when I decided to come clean to her that I had booked an appointment to go round this local woman's house to meet the Pug pups. Now I think there is a part of my wife's brain that thought I was joking, or that "tomorrow" would come and I'd find something else to do. Like, say, coke and hookers. But, no. The following morning, I woke up early and - off I went to, in all honesty, a shit-hole part of town. Hell, I'm not one to judge people or anything but - as I got to the front door, the window was smashed. I was almost tempted to turn away there and then. Had I been there for anything else, such as coke and hookers, I probably would have left but the pull of the puppies was strong!

I knocked the door and a friendly lady opened. I told her I was there to see the puppies and was invited in - whereupon I was set upon by a really hyper mummy Pug called Poppy. She was nuts but *lovely*. Had I been allowed to take her, I probably would have. Especially had I known what puppies were like to train but - we'll get to that later.

Sarah (for that was the lady's name) led me through to the living room. There, in the corner, was a large pen and - within that - a number of little slug-like shapes, all curled up. All sleeping. One little slug, sleeping in the corner by herself. Sarah explained to me that it was Poppy's first litter. She showed me the paperwork showing she was a pedigree and she showed pictures of the dad pug (who didn't live there). Everything looked to be above board but, to be honest, I didn't care about that right at that particular time. I cared about holding the puppies. I asked if it was okay and she said it was but - first - she put Poppy out in the garden so she didn't get upset. Apparently she had an issue with people coming along and grabbing her babies. I don't get it personally. I hate children. If I had one, and someone came along and took it - I'd probably be grateful. Hell, I could sell the story to the papers, do loads of television appearances, write a book, rake the cash in... That's how it's done, isn't it? It all starts with a little holiday to Italy and - away you go: Great holiday, sun, sea, sand, sex and then - a flight home without a screaming kid. Sorry - gone off on a tangent. Moving on, before I get sued...

'She likes to be alone. The others all huddle together but she likes to go off into the corner of the pen by herself,' Sarah said - pointing to the small pup in the corner. Ah ha! A loner, just like me! The perfect companion. We'd be there when we wanted each other but - at the same time - we'd enjoy our own space. (Doesn't work like that, no matter what people tell you, Pugs are like fucking Velcro in the way the little bastards stick to you).

'Can I hold her?' I asked.

Sarah leaned down and picked the sleeping dog up. She didn't stir. I even thought she was dead and was getting ready to ask if there'd be a discount if she was. I held my hand out and Sarah carefully placed the puppy in my hand. Yes, you read that right, in my fucking hand. A little dog... In.... My... Hand.

I asked how old she was. Two weeks. Already I was in love. I mean proper love. I wanted this fucking dog and - without thought - I asked how much she was. The price was confirmed. £1000.00 and the dog was mine, secured with a deposit of £250. She had barely finished the sentence when I told her that I would be back on Sunday with the money - and my wife - if she could "put her to one side" until then. She agreed.

I was thrilled.

My heart skipped a beat. I had secured a little doggie! My first dog! I was officially a dog owner! Without asking half of the questions I needed to ask. Questions - that were - actually pretty important given the fact that I currently rented a home and the paperwork clearly said, *No Pets*. But that's just the little details, right? Who gives a fuck about the little details? I was a dog owner!

All I had to do was tell my wife.

'What time is best to come by on Sunday?' I asked, not even bothered by the fact I was doing all of this without first clearing it with the lady at home.

'Midday would be best.'

I smiled. 'I'll see you then, then!'

Chapter Two.

I have something to tell you.

My wife phoned me on her lunch break. I had not been home long. She asked how my day was and immediately I blurted out that I had gone to see the puppies. Her tone of voice was not of a lady impressed but rather, of one who was concerned and - rightly so - for she knew what an impulsive idiot I can be sometimes. For instance, she went to work one day and by the time she was home - I presented her with tickets for a first class trip to Antigua. A week's vacation for a little over £10,000. That is the potential for damage I have when it comes to what I'm capable of when bored. Admittedly it was a great holiday - one of my best - but that's not the point. It was booked, it still had to be paid for. Similarly, the promise had been made to go back and get the puppy - or rather pay the deposit as she couldn't go home with us until she was a few weeks older - and that too needed to be paid for at a time when I had actual bills to pay. See, the problem with paying bills is they're boring to pay. If companies made it more exciting, like giving you a free toy plastic figure, I'd be more inclined to give them the money they foolishly believe I owe instead of spunking it up the wall elsewhere. *Buy Now, Pay when you feel like it.*

Wifey knew I was being serious when I said we were going back to see the puppies on the Sunday, and that I would be taking her. Immediately her sensible brain kicked in and she started asking question after question after question… Thankfully, before I had left Sarah's home, I too had thought of the questions and - as a result - I had the answers. This was much better than I usually did. Usually I would agree to something and then - when it came to the finer details (such as who would look after it if we wanted another holiday) I would just shrug but - not this time. I *had* the answers and - not just that - I had bloody good answers.

'Who'll look after it when we go on holiday?' she asked.

'Sarah said, so long as we give her enough to cover the food - she will look after her when we go away.'

'Really?'

'Yep.'

'That's good.' (A pause) 'What about the cat?'

The cat was more of an issue. I had rescued her from the Blue Cross and part of that deal was, she couldn't go with other animals because she was a grumpy fuck. I had, however, discussed this with Sarah too.

'If they don't get on, she would take the dog back and give us our money back as she would rather it went to a good home. That being said, she told us we could get a blanket and some toys - that stink of the dog - before we bring the dog home so we can slowly introduce the scent to the home...'

'Really?'

'Yep.'

'That's good.' (A pause) 'What about the costs?'

'I cancel Netflix, which I don't use, and we have this much saved each month. The food costs this much and insurance is this. Spare income currently sits at...'

'Really?'

'Yep.'

'That's good.'

Every question she asked, I was there - like a Ninja - waiting to strike her down and then... I dealt the first of my killer blows.

'I said we would go back on Sunday because you would want to see them too,' I told my wife. I left out the details that I would be handing over a £250 deposit at the same time.

'Oh right. Okay then.'

'Here, if we did have a dog,' I asked... And pay attention for this is the killer of the blows... 'What would you call it?'

<silence>

'Chewie.'

'Really?'

'Yep.'

Chapter Three

"You manipulated me"

The Wife looked at me nervously as she approached the front door to Sarah's house - still completely oblivious to the fact that I had a wad of cash in my back pocket, ready to hand over. I had pre-warned her that it wasn't the best of areas yet, still, she was uncomfortable. I had told her to knock on the door but knew that it would be me that pressed knuckles to wood.

'I'm not knocking,' she said.

See?

I knocked. There was some commotion from inside and the door opened. Sarah was there and - out came Poppy, tail wagging and tongue hanging loosely from her smiley face (pugs smile, get over it). The Wife's face lit up as she bent down to stroke Poppy. I knew I had this in the bag. It was too easy. Like the time I ran up to a small child in the street, stole their ice-lolly, stuck my finger up at them and ran off again laughing like a loon. Ah, good memories.

We walked in and I swear I heard the glass - in the door frame - crack a little more when Sarah closed it behind us. We hung back and she led us through to the living room where - once again - the puppies were sleeping. I was not surprised when The Wife made a bee-line to them without even being asked.

'Can I pick her up?' I asked Sarah. She nodded. She knew I was referring to the little pup with the yellow collar: The dog I had pre-chosen!

I leaned down and collected the puppy from where she slept and I gave her a little cuddle before I told The Wife to hold her hands out. She did. Carefully, like a loving father handing over a baby, I placed the puppy in The Wife's hands. In that instant, I watched her heart melt.

'That's Chewie,' I whispered.

The Wife looked at me and I winked. It was one of those cool moments in the movie where you realise the hero is finally going to get what he wants and clearly deserves. In this case, the hero was me. I was going to get my dog, not that I said anything yet. Instead, I turned to Sarah and reiterated all the questions The Wife had raised the previous day. This way she could hear it straight from the horse's mouth. Not that Sarah was a horse. It's just a saying. Don't ask me where it comes from because, frankly, I don't care enough to waste my time in Googling it for you. Just take my word that it exists. Anyway, we went back through the questions. The Wife then threw almighty curveball.

'What about the landlord?'

Yeah, that was right. We rented the property we were living in at the time and it clearly stated that we weren't allowed pets. I shrugged her answer off though. Fuck him. He had accepted the cat into the house for an extra deposit. He even let us install a cat flap in the back door. We also had three rats which he didn't know about… The way I saw it, the dog was smaller than the cat and less destructive. So long as we respected the property and fixed anything the animals did, what did it matter? Had he said no to the cat (for one, we wouldn't be living there) then it would be a different story but, he said "yes" so clearly didn't mind animals. I calmed the wife's worries by stating we wouldn't let on and that when they did their visits, we would say we were looking after it for my brother. There was nothing in the contracts to state we couldn't do that, after all, and the contract was pretty thick so - if it was a problem I'm sure it would have been said. Anyway, with the pug pup still in her hands quietly snoring, she was just as sold on the idea of getting the dog as I was.

I told her, 'I have the deposit in my pocket.'

We paid the money.

'So what happens next?'

Sarah wrote me out a receipt - at my request - and explained that we couldn't take her home for a few weeks as she was too young and still feeding off her mum's tits. Fair enough, I understand that. It didn't mean I was happy about it though. For those of you who do not know me, patience is not my strong point. We wrote down the collection date and Sarah explained, 'You can come and visit her whenever you want.'

'Really?'

'Yep.'

In hindsight I think Sarah regretted offering that for dog adopters because some of the people took the piss. They'd show up at Sarah's house - sometimes uninvited - and then sit with her for the whole damned evening even though it wasn't always convenient. The Wife and I made do with a flying visit once a week and each visit was torture - not because we didn't like visiting Chewie but because it was hard leaving her there. Again, patience is not my strong point - especially when your puppy is getting cuter with each visit!

1. First visit her eyes were closed.

2. Eyes open and kind of taking things in.

3. Slowly moving around.

4. More pug-like.

5. Eating proper food now!

The Wife and I often reminisce about the first time we visited Chewie, especially in the early days because people would ask how she came to have such a stupid name. The Wife, if you couldn't guess, is somewhat of a Star Wars geek...

Yes, we have a girl dog named after Chewbacca. In her defence though - and forgive me if it is explained within the trilogy - but is Chewbacca actually a dude? I mean, he runs around naked and it's not as though we ever see his penis. Food for thought (him being a her, not his penis).

Upon explaining that The Wife had named the dog without even meeting her, let alone knowing the sex, she would usually turn to me at that point and say, 'You manipulated me into getting that dog.' I just smile when she says it. She's right. I did. I worked her perfectly and - as a result - we got the dog that I had always wanted. The dog that turned out to be a complete and utter bastard but - let's not get ahead of ourselves... We still have the homecoming to look forward to.

Chapter Four

Worse than Christmas Time

If you have a child who wants something, you will know how annoying it is when they want something and keep asking for it. They'll ask for such and such, you will say no, they will then ask again and again and again until one of you explodes. It's one of the most annoying things about children. And me. You see, I'm the same. If I want something, I will keep asking and asking and asking until - finally - I'm allowed it. Just ask The Wife.

'You're a bastard, you said it would just be the tip!' is what she once said when she finally gave in to me pestering her. We'll leave that there. I'll let you figure it out.

Anyway.

Imagine a child asks you for a dog.

'Can we have a dog?'

'Okay.'

'Really?'

'Yep!'

Then explain to that child they have to wait for the dog to come home.

'But why?'

'Because she's not ready to leave her mum yet.'

'So when can she come home?'

'Four weeks...'

'Really?'

'Yep.'

Now the kid knows it has a dog coming. It knows how long it is going to be and yet - every fucking day - that child will ask over and over as to whether the dog is finally coming home. And, when you say it isn't, the child will sulk as though you are the one who has decided the time-frame. Again, I know this because - in this case - I am that child.

Interesting fact: When you put a deposit down on a puppy, the time you have to wait will feel at least three times the *actual* time you have to wait. Now you probably can't compute that in your little brain. It's okay. We can't all be as great as me. But to give you an idea of how bad that is - cast your mind back to when you were a child. Yes, all those years ago. It's December the 1st. Christmas is coming in 24 more days. When you were growing up, and the smell of Christmas hung in the air thanks to the pines of the tree in the living room, how long did those few weeks feel? By some treacherous magic, the month of December felt *longer* - somehow - than January through to August. Waiting to collect your puppy? It's the same. Maybe, somehow, a little worse. Actually, there's a money-making idea: Someone needs to invent a calendar in which you open doors whilst waiting for your puppy to come home. Behind each door could be a doggy treat that you can save up. The final door could be a picture of a kitten. *Surprise, bitches, we couldn't afford a dog - have a cat instead.* Or, better yet, a message that read: "Life is full of disappointments".

I would make a great fucking father.

*

It felt like years from the moment I paid the deposit until the moment I got to pick Chewie up and yet - something I haven't told you - I didn't even have to wait the whole time! Nope. I got her a week early! How awesome was that?! What happened was, I was fast asleep. I can't remember what I was dreaming but my phone woke me up at what I like to call twat o'clock. I looked at the phone and my heart dropped. It was Sarah. Why was she calling me? Had something happened? I answered and she explained that Poppy wasn't well. Basically, she had sore tits. The vet had advised to stop the pups from sucking on them and keep pups and ma separate. Unfortunately, this stressed both the kiddies and the parent. The vet's advice to Sarah was, 'Get the puppies collected early. It's only a week and they're all doing well.' So - yeah - an early morning to collect my dog!

I swear to God I've only ever gotten out of bed at that speed once in my life. Rewind the clock back to when I was a teenager. It was a really hot day, despite being 7am, and the sun was glaring through the window. I had to go to school but had decided the night before that I wasn't going to go. I was going to bunk off around Southampton and catch a film at the cinema instead. So, yeah, knowing I was having my own private (slightly naughty) adventure, I jumped out of bed and packing my rucksack with a change of clothes. I remember that day fondly. Mum dropped me off at the front gate of the school and I walked out of the back. Anyway, none of this is important. What's important was - I was allowed to have my dog early!

'I'll be there in an hour,' I told Sarah, my heart beating joyfully in my chest. My Wife completely unaware of what was happening because she'd already left for work. In my mind, I thought I'd collect Chewie and bring her home and *not* tell The Wife I had her early. Leave it as a surprise until she walked in at the end of the day, only to find me bonding with the puppy without her.

Note: That last sentence sounded a bit pervy. That's not the case. By bonding I just mean that we would be building the foundations for a strong relationship. Of course, it didn't quite work out that way...

Chapter Five
She pissed on me!

I could have got to Sarah's house within twenty minutes. I had told her I would be an hour because - damn it - I needed to go to the shop! I needed to buy a dog bed, dog food, treats and a couple of toys to spoil her with. I mean, I had to! I couldn't just rock up, steal her from her mum, bung her in the car and drive back to my house without anything nice for her. It's a bit - kidnapper.... Or rather, dognapper ish.

Remember at the start when I said dogs are expensive? I spent £60 that day and that was not the end of the costs. Every time I go to the pet store to fetch some food, I end up with treats and toys. Every single time. You would probably say she doesn't need as many toys if you saw them all but I swear to you - she runs to where they are, moves them around until she finds one that she fancies, and then comes running back to me to play too. Another day, it will be another choice. She literally plays with them all. Well nearly. She doesn't touch the big crocodile I bought but then - to be fair - it is bigger than she is. Still, it's the thought that counts right?

So I got to Sarah's house and literally ran to her front door. Once inside she started preparing everything for me. She gave me a blanket that smelt of Poppy (in case Chewie got lonely at night) and she gave me some food, the papers and some little treats - which Chewie was presently too young to enjoy (remember - it's the thought that counts). Sarah got Chewie for me and handed her over.

'Are you ready to come home with me?'

'What? I mean, you're nice but... I'm quite happy here. Besides, I have to look after the dogs.'

'What? No. Not you. I'm talking to Chewie.'

'Really?'

'Yep.'

Okay, that was a lie. None of that was said - other than me asking Chewie if she was ready to come home with me. I was just filling space. You know, giving you value for money and showing you that I'm a little bit weird in the head. The latter being good for when you see me out and about. You'll think to yourself, he's weird in the head and cross the street to get away from me. You see, I don't like people.

Chewie didn't answer my question.

Sarah kept Poppy busy and I made my Great Escape. Once I was in the car, I just sat there cuddling Chewie for a moment. I reassured her the car journey was okay and that she was going to a loving home now. She didn't understand a word but I like to think we bonded a little.

Carefully, I put her in the car dog bed type thing (probably has a proper name but I can't be fucked to find it) and made sure Chewie was secure. I gave her a blanket and put a soft toy in there. Then, I fired up the engine of my car... A short drive (well, about 20 minutes) and we would be home. Except... The Wife worked another 20 minutes down the road in the opposite direction and - well - it felt wrong not to swing by and say hello... A gesture that was kind and certainly not intended to rub it in that I was going home to play with the puppy whilst she was stuck at work for the next seven hours (Please insert an evil laugh here).

So, anyway, I walked in with a smug grin on my face... A puppy cuddled up against my body, cradled in my arms and a flock of women surrounding me. Seriously - if you're a single man reading this - ignore the bad points of my book. Go and buy a puppy. You will drown in pussy. Meanwhile, The Wife, if you've just read that comment - erm.... Fuck off! You don't support my work* anyway so why start with this book?!

   * She does support my work but now she will be more annoyed about that comment than the pussy one. So I saved myself. Sort of. Fuck it, send flowers to my funeral please, I have a feeling it will be a somewhat lonely affair.

   'OH MY GOD! AWWWWWW!' were pretty much the words that came out of The Wife's mouth, and the mouths of her colleagues. A fair reaction given how damned good-looking I am. <sigh, don't crush my dreams> They all flocked around and - being a gent - I handed Chewie over to The Wife for her cuddle. She, of course, responded by doing stupid girly voices to the dog as though that was the way to communicate. Personally, when you talk in a different voice to an animal, I think you're immediately showing the dog you're a bit of a spaz. Talk normally and the dog thinks, *fuck - here is a person who knows shit.* Talk like an idiot and the dog thinks, *Well - this is going to be one easy motherfucker to manipulate.*

   The Wife wanted me to stay all afternoon but she knew I couldn't. It wasn't fair on me. It had been a long day and my legs were tired. It also wasn't fair on Chewie who was confused to Hell and - going by the blinky eyes - tired as fuck. I took her back, after fighting The Wife's colleagues for control of her and took her back to the car after about ten minutes. I secured her and kissed The Wife who was - it's fair to say - insanely jealous that she wasn't coming home with us. Personally speaking, and this is the bastard part of me, I was quite happy she wasn't because I knew we would spend the afternoon fighting over Chewie! I'm not a patient man and I don't really like to share.

   In fact, I don't like to share.

   Chewie was mine.

*

I was lying on the settee. I had collapsed there the moment Chewie and I had got home. She - in turn - collapsed straight on my chest. This cute, tiny little pup snoring soundly - seemingly content in her new environment. Actually she was so tired I don't think she knew where the hell she was. She'd slept most of the way home and she had fallen asleep the moment I put her on my chest after I laid down. I took the opportunity to snap a few photos with the camera and post them up to social media where everyone else declared their love for her. And quite right too.

I'm not sure how long we laid there but it felt like an eternity. Chewie was snoring soundly, occasionally making these funny little squeaks, and I was looking on lovingly - scared to turn the television on for fear of waking her. This moment though, this was why I wanted a dog. Suddenly, she stirred. She opened her eyes and got up on her shaky legs. I cooed and spoke to her in a manly voice and she… She kind of squatted and parted her back legs and… Oh my God… It's so warm… The urine soaked into my tee shirt and trickled down my sides. I'd not even had the damned dog a day yet and she'd already pissed over me. This, as it turns out, was the start of the troubles.

The Obligatory Photo Section

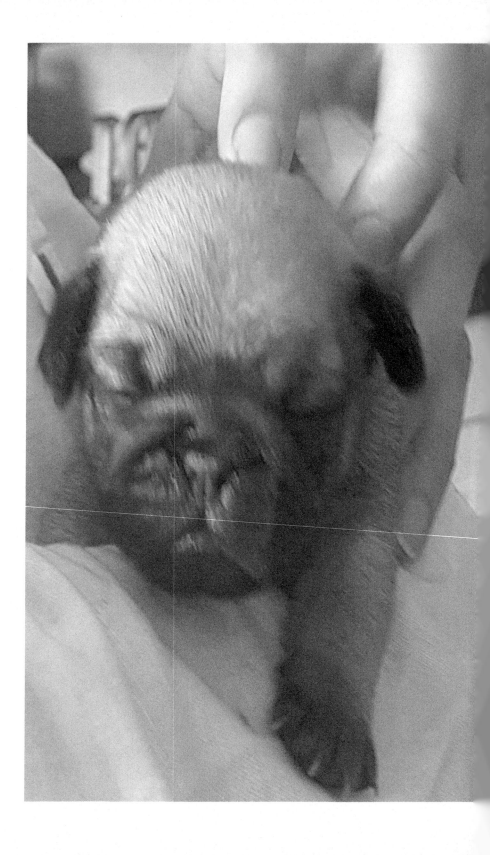

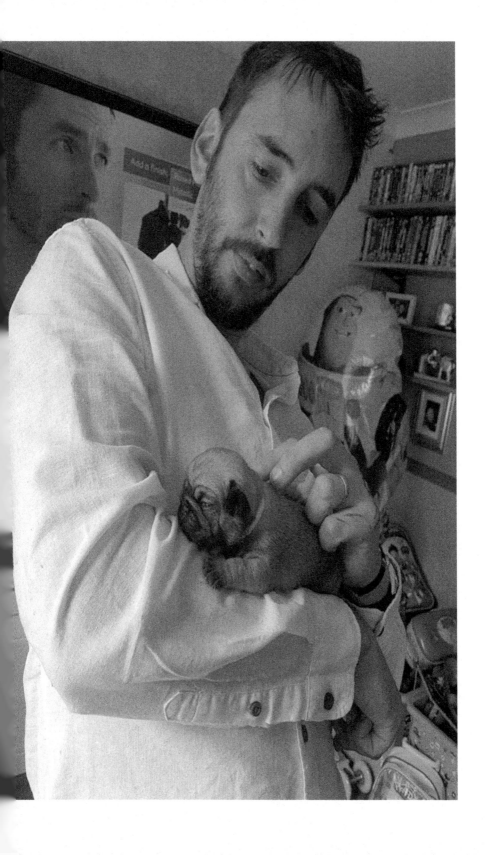

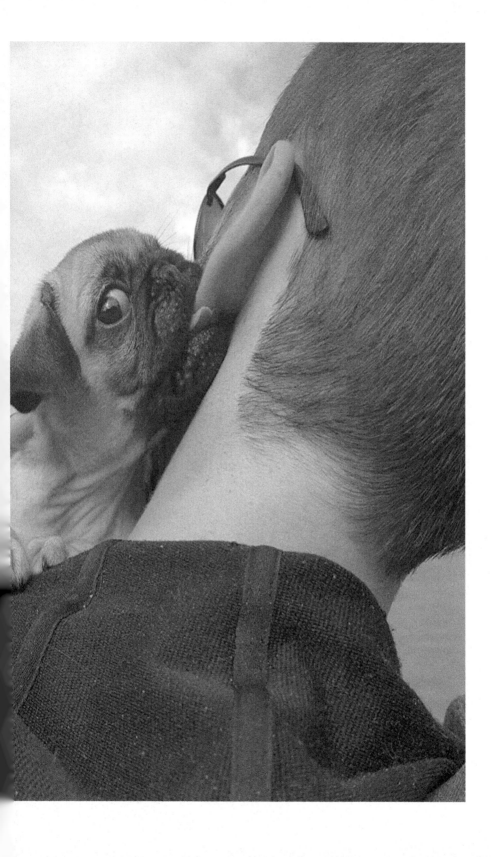

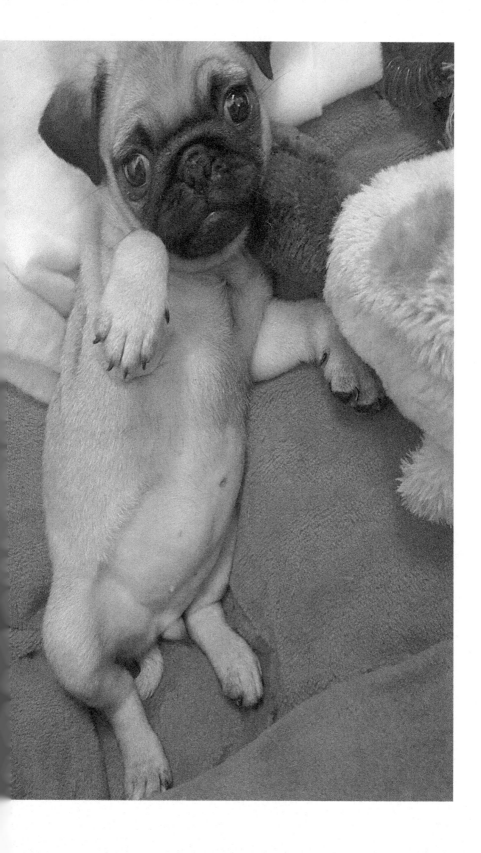

A Change of Pace

The more astute of you (so probably not many - insert a cheeky grin here) might notice the lack of chapter heading for this part of the book. That's because I am mixing it up a little. Instead of going through the rest of my time with Chewie in chapters, detailing how cute she is and how hard it was to get some training done with her - I thought I would just start talking about the various ways in which she is an asshole. For, if I don't, I'm worried some of you will get bored with your low attention spans and skim parts of the book which *might* have had vital information contained within a lovely little anecdote of how cute she is. I say that because I am the same. I'd be reading and think, *not another fucking story about how cute she is,* and then I would skip a couple of pages completely unaware that the middle part of the "cute" story contained a great segment whereby the dog actually jumped onto the kitchen side and took a steaming great shit in the guy's mug of coffee. He - because the coffee was browny-black colour - didn't notice and swigged it right down. Now this hasn't happened to me, it's just an example of what *could* have been missed had I continued the book in the same style as before. For those who did actually skip parts of the earlier job...

Previously in Matt's Life:

Matt got the dog home early because of a medical issue forcing mother dog and puppy dog to be separated. On the way home, he fell in love. This was all he had wanted for at least the last five minutes: A dog of his own. Life was perfect. Before the end of the first day, Chewie repaid Matt's life by pissing all over him in some kind of fucked-up bestiality-watersport scene. And that

wasn't the only issues with bodily functions Matt was to experience.

So there you have it. Now, let's take an in-depth look at how the dog is an asshole and reveal lots of "bastard" things that you most probably didn't think of when you contemplated having a dog. Given we've just been talking about bodily functions - it seems like a logical decision to continue talking about them...

It's all a bit shit (and other gross bodily functions).

In Chewie's defence, she has never shit on me. She has shit next to me, across the room from me, behind me, to the other side of me, in my office, the kitchen, the living room, explosive shit and normal shit in her pen, she's crapped on the floor of the bathroom and she's even dumped repeatedly in my car *but* - she has never shit on me. So, well done Chewie.

Being honest, the crapping was only really a problem for the first few months (6 months, I reckon). Now she knows that - to go outside for a poo - she must ring the bell that hangs by the back door. Same for if she needs to have a piss although this all depends on the mood she is in. If it is raining outside and she thinks she can get away with pissing in the house - I would not put it past her. What makes it frustrating is not that we have to clear it up but rather - she knows it is wrong. It's like, some days, she just wants to annoy us. God only knows the state of the underlay hidden beneath our carpets...

Now I'm actually really forgiving when the dog goes to the toilet in the house because - these days - it has to be for a reason. Also - the worst thing you can do is to shout at them. If you start doing that, they will simply sneak off and do it elsewhere. Little bastards that they are.

It's weird, though, when I think back to wanting a puppy. At no point did I ever stop to think I would have to train her to go outside. The most basic of points and I had completely overlooked it in my excitement of having a canine companion. I mean, I knew I would have to pick up the odd turd when we went on walks but - I didn't think about how many times she would crap in the house or, now she is trained, in the garden. I'll be honest, I just leave it now. Then, once a week, The Wife or I will go out there on a poo-pick-up. Otherwise it's all we would be doing, day in and day out. No thanks.

Anyway, there's another fluid that comes out of dogs too. Again, no one told me about this either but - basically - female dogs get their periods. Yep, that's right, they spend weeks (not days, like women) bleeding. Now, it's loads of blood. The room doesn't look like she has been slashed across the vagina with a knife but that doesn't matter. It's still gross as fuck, made worse by the fact her vagina swelled up. She went from having a fairly tidy one to having her lips hanging so far down I'm surprised she could still walk. It remained like this for about a month. A month of not being able to take her out for a walk, for fear of her getting raped. A month of having her bleeding around the house (and on you). A month of her being annoying because she *wanted* to go out. Before the period was even done, I phoned the vet to get her booked in for the operation to ensure it never happened again. Hey presto, a few weeks after she had finished (as advised) I took her off to the vets and that particular problem was dealt with. It still haunts me though although, sorry to say, we're not done with *this end* of the dog yet. There's yet another damned thing no one told me about and - at the time of writing - I'm dealing with it right now. Any idea? Probably not. This seems to be a secret between dog owners. Well, let me tell you…

Dogs express their anal glands.

Now, I'm not talking about the odd little love puff. This is not a bottom burp. I don't know exactly what it *is* (again, I can't be arsed to Google it) but I do know that it is absolutely rank. And the amount of times she's actually done it on me… Grim. Anyway - let me explain so you can get the full picture. From time to time dogs - for whatever reason - express their anal glands. I guess you could kind of explain it as kind of "scenting" the area. You know it's going to happen because suddenly you are overcome by the fishiest of smells. That's right. Fish. Like, you've walked straight past a fishmongers only - you haven't. Instead, the fishmonger has come to you and literally pissed an invisible fish-juice over you. A stench, so foul, that you *have* to go and change clothes. Otherwise - more so if you're a woman - people will think you have a dirty vagina when they walk by you. You might think I am being crude but that's not the case. We can't deny that the great unwashed does sometimes smell of a rank, out-of-date fish… Weird then, that if you do lick it - it doesn't taste the same. No. It tastes like battery acid. Let me just clarify now, to avoid awkward confusion, I am not talking about the squirt from a dog's anal glands. I have moved, effortlessly, to a dirty woman's foo-foo. How do I know about the taste? I refer you back to the opening part of the book where I make mention of my first girlfriend. More hair than bare. Anyway, I digress.

Supposedly dogs usually express their anal glands when they poo. Sadly, with Chewie, this doesn't seem to be the case. She expresses it when you're dressed, ready to go out for the evening. Maybe it's a little "fuck you" because she doesn't want to be left alone? I don't know. I don't talk "dog" which is why my first relationship failed (see what I did there?). So, yeah, Chewie has soft poo normally which means - the glands don't get squeezed. You *can* do it yourself. What you do, you slide your penis… I'm joking! But, not really. You can do it yourself. You have to put a finger up and… You know what - I don't need to write it because no one who reads this book is going to want to do it themselves. It is disgusting as fuck and you'll end up arguing with your partner as to who's turn it is to take the bastard to the vets.

'I did it last time!'

'Really?'

'Yep!'

'Well fuck off, I'm not doing it!'

'I'll cook for a month.'

'Nope.'

'Two months.'

'And wash up?'

'Yes!'

'No, sorry, I can't do it...'

'And I'll clean the toilet...'

'Not happening.'

'... With my tongue.'

'Okay, tempting. What else?'

Apparently it can be quite painful for the dog, which is a shame. There is an operation they can have to get it removed and sometimes that is a necessary evil. For Chewie - it hasn't come to that yet although, as I type this, I have an appointment in four hours to get her glands expressed again. And, yes, I'm the mug who has to take her. Can not wait (sarcasm here). You're probably wondering what the problem is. The vet does it, not you. That's true. The problem is, you have to hold the dog down so the vet can slip a digit in and - well - there's no way of doing it without having your nose quite close. He expresses the glands, you get a lungful. A smell that you continue to catch whiffs of for the following week.

Oh, and did I mention, if the dog needs help expressing her glands - it's a procedure you have to do fairly often. Not only is it grim but costly as the vet has to do it (at least in my local surgery). His fee? £40 a visit.

Quick Counter Argument to this problem:

I put this segment of the book on Facebook just to gauge reactions, and one of my friends replied, 'My ex expresses anal glands for a living as a dog groomer. This pleases me much more than it should.' I laughed because I know the ex in question and - yeah - they are a complete cunt. So, if anyone ever deserved to do this job for the rest of their life? It's this person. **But**…. It doesn't mean it is worth owning a dog for.

Anyway…

Piss, shit, blood and butt-juice not put you off owning a dog? Read on.

Exercise

When we first got Chewie, we couldn't walk her outside because she hadn't had her jabs and - even when she did have them - we had to wait a while to ensure they were "definitely in her system". It was infuriating because I just wanted to head to the park and immediately play fetch - this being something I've always wanted from a dog. See, although I like cats, they only play one game. It's the "Fuck You" game. You try and get your cat to do something and it looks at you and says, 'Fuck you.' Ah, great game. With a dog I envisioned exploratory adventures in the woods, hunting for treasure. I pictured standing in lush green countryside, up some hill - surveying the area with hand raised to eyes protecting them from the sun. I didn't want to wait for all of this. I'd waited long enough to own the damned dog, why should I wait for *more* things? I had done my waiting! That being said, I didn't want her to get ill so I did as I was told.

During the first weeks we used to go out around town together but I would never put her on the ground because - as said up above - I couldn't. I literally carried her, either cradling her in my arms or with her over my shoulder. Remember when I said dogs were great for attracting the women? When I walked around with the dog like this, the ladies flocked to me. It was great. I would chat and flirt and then - when The Wife approached - be standoffish. Weirdly though, if I walked the dog (still in my arms) and The Wife at the same time - women stayed away but men approached. This was not so great. She went from Chick Magnet to Dick Magnet. I don't know how Chewie did it but it was annoying as fuck. I didn't want dudes approaching. Where's the fun in that? Anyway - when I first wanted a dog, I never thought it would be a good way of meeting *men*. That backfired.

Anyway.

So I was talking about going on exciting walks with the dog. I loved the idea of getting out and about with her and seeing things normally unseen (given the fact I hate walking normally) but I didn't consider the fact that I'd have to take her for a walk even if I didn't actually want to go out for one myself. You know, I'd wake up wanting a lazy day on the sofa with my feet up and shit on the television but Chewie would be running around, itching to go out. Obviously, not being a complete and utter cunt, I would get up and fetch the harness and load up on dog-poo bags and then put my shoes on and find my keys and go to the door and - Chewie doesn't want to go. She's staring out at the pissing rain and then to me, back to the rain, back to me... You can almost hear her say, 'Like fuck am I going out in that.' Now you have two choices, force her out or let her have her own way. Sadly, having come this far, you can't let her back down. You're in charge so you must take her out. You think it will be okay as it is raining and so she will run round the block with you but - that's not the case. She sulks. She drags her feet. She goes painfully slowly to ensure you both get a soaking. And - whilst doing it - she has a really smug look about her face. People laugh when I say that normally. They ask how a dog can have a smug expression. These people are clearly not dog-owners. They're more than likely to be cat-owners. A cat has one expression and that's the "Fuck You" look.

Even on the days where you do want to walk, it still doesn't work out the way you had imagined it. You tend to get a few corners away from the house and then the dog decides to shit. You do the right thing and bag it but then have to carry said bag around because there are no bins anywhere. You just have to complete the walk (until you find one) with a stinking bag of shit hanging in your hand. Actually - this reminds me of a story... And, I swear to you, it's the truth...

So I had gone on a long walk. I say "long walk" but it wasn't that far at all. But, for a pug, it was like running a marathon. As a result, Chewie was walking behind me - lagging behind like a little twat. Now, when I see people walking a bigger dog, I usually make a comment when they approach.

'I've got a snack for your dog.'

I then nod down to Chewie. The other dog owner sees my small dog and then laughs despite knowing - it's probably not a joke. Given half the chance (and certainly if hungry enough) their dog could technically eat mine.

So…

I see a man approaching. He's a skinhead and he has a big dog walking by his side. I don't know the model of the dog. I think it may have been a Ferrari. I don't judge him because he shaves his head. I'm not one of those people. I get ready to say my line. We close the gap. I speak.

'Got a snack for your dog,' I tell him.

He does not look at Chewie. Chewie is hidden behind me. Instead, he looks towards the bag of shit hanging from my hand and then back to me with a look of genuine disgust. It dawns on me what has happened but it's too late - he has now gone past and to shout back would be weird. Instead, I continued walking - thankful that he didn't pound my face in. Not that I am judging him.

'Thanks for that, Chewie!' I said.

I swear to you, I could hear her laughing. I told The Wife the story, recounted it brilliantly too, but she said the dog hadn't been laughing - she was just breathing heavily because she's a pug. Whatever. I know what I heard. My Pug is an asshole.

Anyway, I was side-tracked.

The reason the walks aren't as good as you imagined are because - flip-side of what we spoke about earlier - sometimes you want to go and the dog doesn't. Chewie, instance, will just stop walking. You can try all the bribes under the sun to get her moving but she just won't budge. In the end, much to the anger of other dog-walkers, you just end up dragging her... Her little bum leaving a heavy indentation in the concrete as she wails at you. Okay, that was a slight exaggeration but you get the idea. This is not the only issue that ruins your walks.

Humans.

Humans ruin your walks too.

Let me make this very clear: I don't mind people coming along, with their dogs, and being all friendly. It's nice when you get to stand around (occasionally) and make small talk with people who are out walking their dogs. If anything, it's made me more sociable than I've been in my entire life. Hell, this... This moment right here is part of the fantasy when you think of walking the dog you have not yet purchased. You meet dog walkers, you can fetch, you explore, you get fresh air, you get exercise... It's all good. What I do not like though, is when children come up to you and attempt to pet your dog. Sometimes, they get the dog too excited and other times, they scare the shit out of it. I don't mind so much when they ask, or when their parents tell them to ask but when they just grab... It's times like that I wish I had a massive, child-eating dog as opposed to a slobbering (supposedly overweight) Pug. Also - what are the parents thinking when their child just starts grabbing at a stranger's dog? Do they honestly think that crap is acceptable? Just because a dog looks happy and friendly, doesn't mean it won't just suddenly nip at them and - if it does - who's to blame? The dog and dog-owner, of course. Well, great big hairy lesbian mammoth bollocks to that. A dog bites you? Good. I'm just upset you didn't lose a limb, you snatchy shit. Now, fuck off!

I apologise for the language. It's clearly a subject I feel strongly about. I'm out and about on my walk, these people are ruining it. Oh - and want to know what makes it *even* worse… When strangers come up to you and talk to the dog only. Yep! They ignore you and just talk to your pet in the voice of an idiot. They look and sound so stupid that even the dog is sitting there thinking, 'Who's this cunt?' If you're one of these people - leave us dog walkers alone. You're ruining our walk.

Now you might be thinking that this isn't the dog's fault and it isn't. These people do not make my pug an asshole. What makes my pug an asshole is more to do with the fact that when these people come up to you (and your dog), your pet would rather go home with them! The person greets the dog, you have a brief chat and then they walk off… The dog, with you struggling on the other end of the lead, attempts to go with them despite you shouting SIT and WAIT and STOP and STOP FUCKING MOVING! It's embarrassing. God only knows what the other person is thinking. Probably think we're at home - in the quiet of the evening - beating the dog, hence the desperation for it to get away. I'll be honest, sometimes I just want to let go of the lead and run in the opposite direction.

'Your problem now! Enjoy! She's a cunt!' And you laugh manically into the distance, your middle finger raised. Mind you, I don't know why I am upset about Chewie running off with a stranger… Sometimes it would be nice to have a little time to myself because - damn - this dog should be nicknamed Velcro.

Just Piss Off Already

In my head, owning a dog is brilliant. When you're lonely and need a quick boost - there they are, waiting to cheer you up and fix whatever went wrong in your day. Indeed, my nan had a stroke last year and I was called by her neighbour. I rushed to the house to see her and then went to the hospital. I was there all day with a family member I hadn't spoken to for a few years. It was a tough, tough day. Hang on, that's deep. Let me skip to the end quickly just to say that my nan is fine now (weaker but she is talking and walking) and bridges were built between myself and said family member so - happy days. Okay, back to the actual day. The day was long, stressful and I could barely stop myself crying as I drove home due to worry over my nan and the buried feelings between myself and the family member. In short - I felt terrible. When I got home though, there was little Chewie (about 3 months old at that point) and - boy - was she pleased to see me! The moment I stepped over the threshold, she came bounding down the hallway, tail wagging. I picked her up and cradled her in my arms as she demanded belly rubs and squirmed around with excitement. In short: She lifted my spirits right up. Now *that* is what I envisioned owning a dog would be like and - for the most part - it is. But, it's not that simple… Why? Because, sometimes you just want some peace and quiet. A little space to yourself - if only for a wank.

Right, I'm not sure about other dogs. I have no experience with them. What I am about to say, though, is very much a trait of pugs. They are - to put it simply - velcro. They just stick to you. Doesn't matter what you're doing, they want to be a part of it. On the one hand, it's lovely and - on the other - seriously, just sod off. Even going to the toilet offers you no reprieve but we will get to that in a minute.

All day I have this dog pestering me, begging to eat the food I am enjoying and generally just giving me no peace and quiet. It's frustrating. So - when The Wife comes home - I am grateful as fuck. I think, *finally, I get some time to myself.* The Wife, however, has had a hard day at work and wants a few minutes to unwind. Maybe even do a little work out routine (for some weird reason she thinks this is a good way to unwind when, really, we all know a wank is the answer). Anyway, she walks in and it goes something like this:

'Oh good, you're home!' I hand the dog over.

'What? I want to go and do a work out.'

'Well how long for?!'

'An hour?'

'Really?'

'Yep.'

'I've had this fucking dog all day…'

At which point she explodes about having been out of the house since 6am that morning. I then counter-argue that I've been working hard all day too - or trying at least - but not got half of what needed to be done because of the fucking dog. She storms off, doors slam. At no point in my dreams of dog owning did I ever stop to consider arguments. Still - fast forward a little… She's done her workout, you've had some time to yourself and now you're both on the settee, chilling out. The dog between you. You try and reach an arm around. The dog is there. You wink to The Wife hoping she recognises the signs you're up for some adult fun and - the dog winks back. You stick your tongue out towards the wife and flap it around wildly - teasing her that you're in the mood for a spot of muff-diving and - that asshole dog sticks its tongue out. My pug is an asshole because not only does it stress me out during the day but it also causes arguments and kills the sex life. Hell, we might as well have had a child.

Anyway.

Toilet business. You leave the door open because, if you don't, the little bastard ruins the door. Unfortunately - leaving the door open - this leaves you taking a wee, or dump, with a dog looking at you - wondering what the hell you're doing.

I've been giving this some thought. As much as it annoys me, I don't think the dog can really be blamed for how it acts in this situation. The reason being, when you take the dog out for a poo, or wee, you tend to stand there waiting. Sometimes you can even find yourself standing there, watching them - urging them to go. So basically - when you go to the toilet - they're just copying what you do when they go. To them, you see, it is normal. We have made the dogs think like that. unfortunately, when in my garden, I can't not watch my dog because the little bitch will often take leave under the fence which brings me to another reason my pug is an asshole.

<u>Chase Me!</u>

You're standing in the field. You throw the ball. The dog chases, grabs it, runs back to you and drops the ball at your feet. It looks at you (the dog, not the ball - don't be weird) lovingly. Its tongue hangs out as it pants (the dog, not the tongue - do I really need to explain this?). You collect the ball and throw it again. The dog is already setting off for it.

'I love you, best friend!'

'I love you too,' the dog doesn't reply because it can't actually speak but would definitely say something like this if it could. And, for the rest of the afternoon, you play lovingly. Except the reality doesn't work like that. The reality is irritating as fuck.

The dog fetches the ball. That bit works. The dog grabs it, comes back and stops by your feet. Good girl! You bend down but the ball is not dropped from the dog's mouth. Instead, the dog backs away from you.

'No, drop it.'

She doesn't though.

'Drop it!'

You reach again, the dog backs away.

'Drop it you little shit.'

You reach. The dog runs.

'Get back here, you fucking turd!'

The dog is now running circles around you. Literal circles with its mouth clamped around the ball. Meanwhile - other dog walkers are watching sympathetically. They've been here before and it's only changed (for them) now their dog is old and can't be bothered to play the "game" anymore. I'm telling you:

Dogs are assholes. And… And don't think it's just this (the balls) they make you chase them for. They have another, equally annoying habit. Or rather, Chewie does at least.

Picture the scene:

My Wife comes home from a hard day at work. It's been hot. It's been sweaty. She wants a shower. So far, so good. I'm in the kitchen cooking dinner (seriously, The Wife can't cook) and suddenly Chewie runs by. She's panting in a way I immediately recognise. She has a mouthful. I look to see what she has got - after all, she has been quiet for a while now and that always means trouble - and, oh look, she has stolen The Wife's day-old knickers.

'Chewie!' I shout.

By now she has stopped running and collapsed in a heap. By now, she is munching on the moist gusset of said knickers. I go to get the knickers off her and - yep - she grabs them, gets up and runs off. Once, even, the backdoor was open and the little twat ran straight out and into the garden. If the neighbours look out of their window at this point, they would have seen me chasing the dog around, fist raised in anger and the dog not giving a flying fuck.

Gone are the days when The Wife gets home from work and jumps into the shower whilst I sneak into the room and have a sniff of her… Sorry, what? Forget I said anything. Move on. Nothing to see. In fact no, I'm not ashamed. Sometimes a guy just wants to, you know… Be closer to The Wife (or any female for that matter) and if the closest he can get is a pair of dirty knickers then so be it, by Jove! Anyway, regardless of a person's tastes… No one thinks about having to fight a dog for a pair of dirty knickers when they're considering becoming a dog owner. It's just not one of those things that factor into the thoughts, you know? You think about playing fetch, cuddling, walking - not fighting over crusty cacks! What makes it worse is, even if you're quick and get them back fast, they're still fucking ruined. A gusset of moist-goodness now one filled with dog spit. Hardly something you want to stick your nose into, is it? I mean, unless you're a fucking weirdo.

Oh - and speaking of weirdos.

Believe it or not but we did do training with Chewie. The woman was as useful as a water resistant sponge but - at least we tried. This woman - we shall refer to her as Dragon for that is how I feel about her - was an absolute twat. She was self-righteous and a proper money-grabber. During the class, we were told to put our hands up if we needed anything or were having troubles. We did. She would always tell us we needed a home-visit so we could go through the problems properly. Of course - that meant a fuck ton more money. Like I said, money-grabbing Dragon.

Still - she informed us of the time she was sitting in the living room when her dog came bounding in with a sex toy in its mouth. Apparently the dog had found the toy in the bedroom and - well… By now, if you're like me and have pictured the Dragon properly, you'll be vomiting blood so we will leave that right there, yeah? The point is, though, that clearly it's a common problem: Dog's steal shit that doesn't belong to them and then make you chase them around until you're able to get it back (or they've eaten it). Dogs are dicks.

Oh - one positive though… If you do happen to get to your partner's pants before they put them in the wash or the dog gets them, they're yours for good. You see, your partner will come out of the shower and go to pick up the dirty clothes scattered around. They don't know this, you've already stashed the pants.

'You seen my pants?'

'Think the dog had them.'

'Really?'

'Yep!'

'For fuck sake…'

You turn away from your partner and unleash a crafty smile… You evil genius you. Still doesn't excuse it completely though. You'll lose more cacks to the dog than you'll gain for yourself. That's the way the cookie crumbles and, speaking of cookie's and crumbs…

<u>Manipulative Bastards</u>

Meal times are ruined when you get a dog. Even if you feed your dog at the same time, they tend to wolf their food so fast that they'll be done long before you've finished munching upon your first potato. Do they sit there and patiently wait for you to finish yours? Or maybe they go off and entertain themselves for a while - allowing you time to digest your dinner? Do they fuck. They waddle over and sit by your feet - staring up at you with puppy-dog eyes. Occasionally they'll shuffle their feet forward ever so slightly, or they'll make a bit of a whining noise - you know, just to be sure you've seen them there. If you have already gone out and bought a dog and are just waiting for it to arrive into your life - take my words very seriously - **do not** look your dog in the eye whilst you try and eat. It is impossible not to give them scraps and - once you've done that - you've lost the game. Whenever you try and eat something, the dog will be there fully aware that you're a soft touch. To this day I can't eat in peace and I can't remember the last time I had any snacks without having to snap a bit off for the dog. What makes the whole damned thing even more annoying is I'm the one who is treated like a criminal when I go to the vets.

'Your dog is overweight,' they say as they eyeball you suspiciously.

'Really?'

'Yep.'

'It's not my fault. I go out for the day and she sneaks herself a sandwich.'

'Uh huh.'

'It's true. I once came home and found her cooking a full on roast.'

Tell you what - all this talk of food… I went to the Pet Store today, to grab her some biscuits, and I ended up buying more toys and - of course - treats (because that'll really help with the diet the vet put her on, I'm sure). As I type this, I find myself gagging and my eyes burning. She absolutely stinks as she occasionally lets slip with a fart that literally sounds like air escaping from a tyre. Or, sometimes (and far more treacherous), there is no noise at all. Actually, bollocks to this, I'm gagging her. Time to call it a night and go to my bed whilst I'm still able to breath. I can pick this up again in the morning.

*

Chewie's stomach has settled. Thank God. Here, I was thinking about her farts last night and there is one benefit to them. Usually they are silent. This means they catch you unaware and you cop a lungful before you know what has happened. It's disgusting but you can use it to your advantage… If you let out a silent guff yourself (or "love puff" as my wife calls it… At least, when she does it) you can, nine times out of ten, blame it on the dog. Well I can anyway because I'm a little more beefy. My wife can't blame the dog because she is a little more "ready-salted" flavour. Very distinct. Anyway, there is that little point to consider when bringing a dog into your life: You can blame your bottom burps on them. In fact, they're quite useful really, when you really think about it.

'Gross! The dog farted again!' (stifle laughter as partner chokes)

'The dog must have stolen your knickers. Dirty bitch.'

'I didn't eat it. Must have been the dog.'

And before you think I am an evil bastard for blaming everything on the dog, keep in mind the title of this section: "Manipulative Bastards". See it doesn't matter what a dog does. It could shit in your brand new shoes, it could rape your wife… The fact of the matter is - dogs are capable of giving you a look which melts your heart and turns you into mush. You go from being really angry to thinking, *awwww you're so cute* before declaring your love for them. Nine times out of ten you don't even realise it has happened until it is too late and then - well - it's too late! The dog wins! I guess that's why I am sitting here now thinking that my pug isn't actually the asshole I initially stated she was when I first started this book. She's looking at me and - you'll think I am crazy - I am sure she is smiling. She's kind of cute, in an ugly kind of way. Her little snores are endearing and I love how she depends on me. She loves me unconditionally, even when I am in a foul mood - she is there to cheer me up and remind me that, actually, the world isn't that bad. In fact, the more I think about it, the more I think that maybe I'm the asshole for penning this book in the first place. I'm the bad guy, not her. She's innocent in all of this. She's…

… Just manipulated me with the puppy dog look. For fuck sake, I fell for it again. I stand by my original statement: My Pug is an asshole and - with that - I am done.

In all seriousness though

Chewie is a nob, there is no mistaking that. She has lots of quirks (like barking at her reflection in the television screen) and likes to test my patience most of the time but there is truth in what I stated in the earlier paragraph, hinting that I love her. I do love her. I just came into the dog-owning world unprepared and whilst this book is written with tongue firmly in cheek - I hope it has raised some issues to you, the wannabe dog owners, that there are some things you need to be aware of before investing in a dog. If you know everything, the good and the bad - you can make an informed decision and go out and get a dog of your own. Or, you can realise, it's not for you and you can get - oh I don't know - a cat instead. Which brings me to the blatant advert for the second book: My Cat is a Cunt... Nah, I'm joking. I don't need to write that as a book. Everyone knows what cats are like. The point I am trying to make is: If you want a pet, do all of your homework before you go and buy one. Make sure it is right for you. Don't be one of those assholes who gets one and then gives up on it because it annoys you from time to time. At the end of the day, they're not just pets. They're little beings who are trying to live a happy life and everyone deserves to be happy. If you disagree with that statement, do not get a pet because - in case you can't see it in yourself - you're a selfish prick. Now, if you don't mind, I have to go and hug my asshole pug.

Made in the USA
Las Vegas, NV
22 December 2020